I am lāt_e. I āt_e ham on a hill.

I āt_e and āt_e. and now I am

lāt_e. I will run.

I wish I had sand. I wish I had a rāk_e. I wish I had a fish.

I wish I had a lāk_e.

hē has a fat cat. hē has fun

with his fat cat.

his mom has a littlₑ cat. shē

has fun with thē littlₑ cat. thē

littlₑ cat has fun in thē sand.

a littl_e fish sat on a fat fish.

thē littl_e fish said, "wow."

thē littl_e fish did not hāt_e thē

fat fish. thē littl_e fish said,

"that fat fish is mom."

thē cow sat on a gāt_e. thē cow said, "thē gāt_e is hot." shē said, "I hāt_e hot gāt_es."

a fish āt_e a roc_k. thē fish

said, "I āt_e a roc_k."

a cow āt_e thē fish. thē cow

said, "I āt_e a fish. and now I

fēēl sic_k."

shē can kick. shē can lick. shē

said, "I am not a cat." shē said,

"I am not a fish."

is shē a man?

shē was not mad at him. did

shē hit him? nō, nō, nō. did shē

hug him? nō, nō, nō. did shē

kiss him?

hē said, "can I ēₐt a nut?"

shē said, "gō sit with thē

cow."

hē said, "nō. I will not gō."

shē said, "gō sit with thē cat."

hē said, "thē cat can ēₐt a nut."

shē said, "gō sit with thē cat

and ēₐt."

sō hē ātₑ a nut. hē said, "this is

fun."

hē has nō fēēt. hē has nō

nōse. hē has nō tēēth. hē is not

a cow. and hē is not a cat.

is hē a rat? nō. hē is not a

rat.

I can kiss a cat. I can kiss

a kitt_en.

can a cow kiss mē? nō. a cow

can not kiss mē. a cow can

lic_k mē.

can a cat lic_k a kitt_en?

I havₑ a cow. thē cow is fat.

I havₑ a cat. thē cat is fat.

how can I tākₑ thē cow and

thē cat with mē? can thē cow

sit on thē cat? nō.

wē havₑ hats. I can hōld thē

hats. thē cow can hōld thē hats.

an ōld man can hōld thē hats.

can a fat rat hōld thē hats?

wē sāve rocks. wē sāve sacks

and sacks of rocks. wē sāve

lots and lots of rocks.

wē have lots of little rocks.

wē sit on rocks. and wē give

an ōld man lots of rocks.

thē ōld man said, "I can shāve a cat." sō hē did.

thē ōld man said, "I can shāve a cow." sō hē did.

thē ōld man said, "I can shāve a rock."

did hē shāve a rock? nō.

hē said, "givₑ mē a hat ōr a socₖ." sō shē gāvₑ him a socₖ fōr his nōsₑ.

hē said, "I nēēd socₖs on thē fēēt, not on thē nōsₑ." sō shē gāvₑ him socₖs fōr his fēēt.

thē ōld man was cōld. hē did

not havₑ a hat ōr a cōₐt ōr socₖs.

sō hē got a gōₐt with lots of

hats and cōₐts and socₖs.

now thē ōld man is not cōld

and thē gōₐt is not cōld.

the ōld gōat had an ōld cōat.

the ōld gōat said, "I will ēat this

ōld cōat." sō she did.

"that was fun," she said. "I āte

the ōld cōat. and now I am cōld."

now the ōld gōat is sad.

the fat man and his fat cow

got on a little rock.

a cat said, "fat man, that rock

will not hold a fat man and his

cow. that rock will go down

the hill."

did thē rocₖ gō down thē hill

with thē fat man and his fat

cow?

thē rat had fun. hē ran in

thē sand.

hē had sand on his fēēt. hē

had sand on his ēars. hē had

sand on his nōse. hē had sand

on his tāil.

hē said, "I havₑ a lot of sand ⟶

on mē." ⟶

shē said, "I haVe a fan."

hē said, "I haVe sand."

shē said, "wē can run thē

sand in thē fan." sō hē ran thē

fan nēar thē sand.

hē had sand in his ēars. hē

said, "I can not hēar."

hē had sand on his sēat. shē

said, "wē havₑ sand on us."

a dog sat in a little car. thē

dog said, "I nēēd to ēat."

will thē dog ēat a fish? nō.

will thē dog ēat a log? nō. will

thē dog ēat a pot of tar? nō.

thē dog will ēat thē car.

a dog was in thē fog. a cat

was in thē fog. a gōat was in

thē fog.

thē dog and thē cat and thē

gōat cāme to a log.

thē cat and thē dog sat on thē

log. thē dog and thē cat said,

"wē arₑ on thē log."

thē gōₐt said, "I am not on

thē log. I am in thē log. ha ha."

thē fat man and his *dog* had

a car. thē car *did* not run.

sō thē fat man and his *dog*

got a gōat. thē fat man and

his *dog* sat on thē gōat. thē gōat

did not gō.

thē fat man said, "thē gōat will not gō."

sō thē fat man and his dog sat on thē rōad.

lots of cars

a man on a farm has lots of

cars. hē has ōld cars. hē has

littlₑ cars.

arₑ his cars fōr gōₐts? nō.

arₑ his cars fōr shēēp? nō. arₑ

his cars fōr cows? nō.

his cars arₑ fōr cops. hē has

lots of cop cars.

thē girl and thē dog

thē girl said, "I can tēach thē dog to run."

thē dog said, "nō."

thē girl said, "I will tēach thē

dog to run."

the dog said, "no. the girl can

not teach me to run. I can run.

ha ha."

a girl in a cāve

a girl was in a cāve. a wāve
cāme in thē cāve. thē girl said,
"sāve mē, sāve mē."
a fish cāme in thē cāve. she

said, "I will sāvₑ that girl."

and shē did.

the fish said, "now I will givₑ

that girl a sēēd and a ham to

ēat." sō shē gāvₑ thē girl a sēēd

and a ham.